085
7

LITTLE LENIN

VOLUME

D1622694

THE TASKS OF
THE PROLETARIAT
IN OUR REVOLUTION

By V. I. LENIN

INTERNATIONAL PUBLISHERS
381 FOURTH AVENUE · NEW YORK

THE TASKS OF
THE PROLETARIAT
IN OUR REVOLUTION

BY

V. I. LENIN

MARTIN LAWRENCE, LTD.
LONDON

EDITOR'S FOREWORD

LENIN arrived in Petrograd from his exile in Switzerland April 16, 1917. The following day he presented his views at a meeting of Bolshevik members of the national conference of Soviets of Workers' and Soldiers' Deputies in the form of theses published afterward under the title "The Tasks of the Proletariat in the Present Revolution" (pp. 32-36). These theses, known in Bolshevik annals as the "April Theses," were in the main a succinct formulation of the views expressed in his "Letters from Afar." (See Little Lenin Library, Vol. 8.)

A more rounded out presentation of his position on the various national and international problems arising out of the Russian Revolution and the imperialist war, Lenin gave in "The Tasks of the Proletariat in Our Revolution," written also in the form of theses and offered by him as a "platform of a proletarian party" (pp. 3-31). The principles and tactics enunciated by Lenin in this "platform" guided the strategy and action of the Bolsheviks during the transition from the bourgeois revolution in March to the proletarian revolution in November.

Lenin met with opposition among some Bolsheviks, particularly on the part of L. B. Kamenev, who disagreed fundamentally with his thesis regarding the nature of the revolution and the direction it must take. The question at issue was whether the bourgeois revolution had already completed its course and the prerequisites for its transition into the proletarian revolution were at hand. Lenin took up this basic point of difference in his "Letters on Tactics" (pp. 37-48), which together with the other writings included in this booklet served as the basic material for discussion on the eve of the national conference of the Bolshevik Party early in May (see Little Lenin Library, Vol. 10) at which the final policies and tactics were to be hammered out.

A. T.

THE TASKS OF THE PROLETARIAT IN OUR REVOLUTION

PROPOSED PLATFORM OF A PROLETARIAN PARTY

THE historical moment through which we are passing is characterised by the following fundamental traits:

THE CLASS CHARACTER OF THE REVOLUTION

1. The old tsarist power, which represented only a handful of feudal landowners in command of the entire state machinery (army, police, bureaucracy) has been shattered and removed, but not entirely destroyed. The monarchy has not been formally abolished. The Romanov coterie continues monarchist plots. The vast estates of the feudal landowners have not been liquidated.

2. State power in Russia has passed into the hands of a new class, namely, the bourgeoisie and the bourgeoisified landowners. To *that* extent the bourgeois-democratic revolution in Russia has been completed.

Finding itself in power, the bourgeoisie formed a bloc with openly monarchist elements which became notorious by their unusually ardent support of Nicholas the Bloody and Stolypin the Hangman in 1906-1914 (Guchkov and other politicians to the right of the Cadets). The new bourgeois government of Lvov and Co. has attempted to negotiate with the Romanovs concerning the restoration of the monarchy in Russia. While shouting revolutionary phrases, this government has appointed partisans of the old régime to positions of authority. Having turned over the entire state machinery (army, police, bureaucracy) to the bourgeoisie, this government strives to reform it as little as possible. The revolutionary initiative of mass action and the seizure of power by the people from below, this only assurance of a real success of the revolution, already meets with all sorts of obstacles on the part of the new government.

The government has not as yet announced the date for the convocation of the Constituent Assembly. Neither does it touch the

3

ownership of the landed estates, this material foundation of feudal tsarism. The government does not even contemplate starting an investigation of the activities, or making public the activities, or controlling the monopolistic financial organisations of the large banks, the syndicates and cartels of the capitalists, etc.

The main and decisive ministerial posts in the new government (the ministry of the interior, the war ministry, *i. e.,* the command over the army, the police, the bureaucracy and the entire machinery for the oppression of the masses) belong to notorious monarchists and adherents of the large landholding system. The Cadets, those republican since yesterday, republicans against their will, have been given posts of secondary importance, in no way connected with authority over the people and with the machinery of state power. A. Kerensky, a representative of the Trudoviks * and "also a Socialist," does literally nothing else but lull to sleep the people's watchfulness and attention with well-sounding phrases.

For all these reasons, the new bourgeois government does not deserve the proletariat's confidence even in the field of internal politics, and no support of it is admissible on the part of the workers.

THE FOREIGN POLICIES OF THE NEW GOVERNMENT

3. In the domain of foreign policy, which was placed in the forefront in consequence of objective conditions, the new government stands for the continuation of the imperialist war waged in concert with the imperialist powers, England, France, and others, for the sake of sharing capitalist spoils, for the sake of strangling small and weak peoples.

Dominated by the interests of Russian capital and its powerful protector and master, Anglo-French imperialist capital, which is the wealthiest in all the world, the new government, despite the wishes expressed most definitely in the name of a clear majority of the Russian peoples through the Soviet of Workers' and Soldiers' Deputies, has taken no real steps whatever towards stopping the slaughter of peoples for the interests of the capitalists. It has not even published the secret treaties of a frankly predatory character (concerning the partition of Persia, the robbing of China, the robbing of Turkey, the annexation of East Prussia, the annexation

* A parliamentary group primarily of peasant deputies under the influence of the Socialist-Revolutionary Party.—*Ed.*

4

of the German colonies, etc.) which, as everybody knows, bind Russia to Anglo-French imperialist and predatory capital. It has confirmed these treaties concluded by tsarism which for several centuries robbed and oppressed more peoples than did all other tyrants and despots, tsarism which not only oppressed but also disgraced and demoralised the Great-Russian people by transforming it into an executioner of other peoples.

The new government, having confirmed those shameful and predatory treaties, has not offered to all the belligerent peoples an immediate armistice, in spite of the clearly expressed demands of a majority of the peoples of Russia voiced through the Soviets of Workers' and Soldiers' Deputies. It has evaded the issue by resorting to solemn, sonorous, glittering but perfectly empty phrases and declarations, which have always served, and do serve, in the mouths of bourgeois diplomats to deceive the gullible and naïve masses of an oppressed people.

4. This is why the new government not only does not deserve the slightest confidence in the domain of foreign policy, but even to demand of it that it should make known the will of the peoples of Russia for peace, that it should renounce annexations, etc., would, in reality, mean to deceive the people, to awaken in them hopes that cannot be realised, to retard their intellectual enlightenment, indirectly to reconcile them to a continuation of a war of which the social character is determined not by good wishes but by the class character of the government that wages the war, by the alliance between the class represented by that government and the imperialist finance capital of Russia, England and France, etc., by that real and actual policy which that class conducts.

UNIQUE DUAL POWER AND ITS CLASS MEANING

5. The main peculiarity of our revolution, a peculiarity most urgently requiring thoughtful analysis, is dual power established during the very first days after the victory of the revolution. This dual power is expressed in the existence of two governments: one is the main, real, actual government of the bourgeoisie, the "Provisional Government" of Lvov and Co. which has in its hands all the organs of power; the other is an additional, a parallel, a "controlling" government, the Petrograd Soviet of Workers' and Soldiers' Deputies, which has no organs of state power in its hands,

but which is based directly on a clear majority of the people, on the armed workers and soldiers.

The class origin and the class meaning of this dual power is to be found in the fact that the March Revolution has not only swept away the entire tsarist monarchy, has not only transferred all power to the bourgeoisie, but has also come close to a revolutionary-democratic dictatorship of the proletariat and the peasantry. Precisely such a dictatorship (that is, power resting not on law but on the direct force of armed masses of the population) and precisely of the above-mentioned classes is the Petrograd and other local Soviets of Workers' and Soldiers' Deputies.

6. The second highly important feature of the Russian Revolution is the circumstance that the Petrograd Soviet of Soldiers' and Workers' Deputies, which obviously enjoys the confidence of most of the local Soviets, voluntarily transfers state power to the bourgeoisie and its Provisional Government, voluntarily surrenders to the latter its own supremacy after having entered into an agreement to support it, and limits itself to the rôle of a supervising body assuring the convocation of the Constituent Assembly (the date for the convocation of which has not as yet been announced by the Provisional Government).

This most peculiar situation, unparallelled in history, has led to the simultaneous existence and interlocking of two dictatorships: the dictatorship of the bourgeoisie (for the Provisional Government of Lvov and Co. is a dictatorship, *i. e.*, power based not on law nor on a previously expressed will of the people, but on seizure by force, which seizure was accomplished by a definite class, namely, the bourgeoisie) and the dictatorship of the proletariat and the peasantry (the Soviet of Workers' and Soldiers' Deputies).

There is not the slightest doubt but that such a combination cannot last long. There can be no two powers in a state. One of them is bound to dwindle to nothing, and the entire Russian bourgeoisie is already straining all its energies everywhere and in every possible way in an endeavour to weaken, to set aside, to reduce to nothing the Soviet of Workers' and Soldiers' Deputies, to create one single power for the bourgeoisie.

Dual power expresses merely a transition moment in the development of the revolution, when it has gone farther than the usual bourgeois-democratic revolution, but has not yet reached a "pure" dictatorship of the proletariat and the peasantry.

The class meaning (and class explanation) of this transitional, unstable situation consists in the following: Like every other revolution, our revolution demanded the greatest heroism and self-sacrifice on the part of the masses in the struggle against tsarism, and all at once it set in motion an unusually large number of people.

One of the chief symptoms, from the point of view of science and practical politics, of every real revolution is the unusually brusque, sharp and sudden increase in the number of the average run of people who begin to participate, actively, independently, and forcefully, in political life, in the state apparatus.

This is the case of Russia. Russia is now in a state of ebullition. Millions of people, politically asleep for ten years, politically crushed by the terrible pressure of tsarism and slave labour for landowners and manufacturers, have awakened and thrown themselves into politics. Who are these millions of people? Mostly small proprietors, petty-bourgeois, people half way between capitalists and wage workers. Russia is the most petty-bourgeois of all the European countries.

A gigantic petty-bourgeois wave has swept everything, has overwhelmed the class-conscious proletariat not only numerically but also ideologically, *i. e.*, it has infected, it has captured very wide circles of workers with the political ideals of the petty bourgeoisie.

The petty bourgeoisie, in real life, depends upon the bourgeoisie; living, as it does, not like proletarians, but like property-owners (as far as its position in social production is concerned), it also follows the bourgeoisie in its way of thinking.

An attitude of unreasoning confidence in the capitalists, the worst foes of peace and Socialism,—such is at present the attitude of the Russian masses, such is the feeling that has grown with revolutionary rapidity out of the socio-economic soil of the most petty-bourgeois country of Europe. Such is the class basis for the "agreement" existing between the Provisional Government and the Soviet of Workers' and Soldiers' Deputies (I emphasise that I have in mind not so much formal agreement as practical support, tacit understanding, a naïvely trustful yielding of power)—an agreement that has given to the Guchkovs a fat morsel, actual power, whereas to the Soviet it gave promises, honour (for the time being), flattery, phrases, assurances, curtsies on the part of the Kerenskys.

The insufficient numerical strength of the proletariat in Russia, its insufficient class-consciousness and organisation—this is the reverse of the same medal.

All the Narodnik parties,* including the Socialists-Revolutionists, have always been petty-bourgeois. The same is true of the party of the Organisation Committee † (Chkheidze, Tsereteli, etc.) ; the independent revolutionists (Steklov and others) have equally drifted with the tide, at least they have not overcome it, they have had no time to overcome the tide.

The Peculiarity of the Tactics Following from the Above

7. From the peculiarity of the actual situation indicated above follows the peculiarity of present tactics, which are obligatory for a Marxist who reckons with objective facts, with masses and classes, rather than with persons, etc.

This peculiarity makes it imperative "to pour vinegar and bile into the sweetish water of revolutionary democratic eloquence" (as a fellow member of the Central Committee, Teodorovich, expressed himself—most aptly—at yesterday's session of the All-Russian Congress of Railroad Employés and Workers in Petrograd). We must do the work of criticism, expose the mistakes of the petty-bourgeois Socialist-Revolutionist and Social-Democratic parties, prepare and weld together the elements of a class-conscious proletarian Communist Party, free the proletariat from the spell of the "common" petty-bourgeois delusion.

In appearance this is "nothing more" than propaganda work. In reality, this is the most practical revolutionary work, for a revolution cannot possibly be moved forward when it stalls, it chokes on phrases, it treads everlastingly the same spot not because of outside obstacles, not because the bourgeoisie uses force (so far Guchkov only threatens to use force against the soldiers), but simply by the unthinking confidence of the masses.

Only by combating this unthinking confidence (and one can and must combat it only ideologically, by comradely persuasion, by

* Populists.—*Ed.*

† The Central Committee elected at the 1912 Conference was the organisational centre of the Bolsheviks, while the Organisation Committee was that of the Mensheviks.—*Ed.*

8

reference to life's experience) can we free ourselves from the reigning bacchanalia of revolutionary phrases and make real progress in stimulating the class-consciousness of the proletariat and of the masses in general, as well as their determined initiative everywhere, their self-willed realisation, development and strengthening of liberties, democracy, and the principle of national ownership of all the land.

8. The world-wide experience of bourgeois and feudal governments has developed two methods of keeping people enslaved. The first is violence. Nicholas Romanov I, called Nicholas Palkin,* and Nicholas II, the Bloody, showed to the Russian people a maximum of what is possible and impossible in the use of this, the hangman's method. But there is another method, the one best developed by the English and French bourgeoisie, who were "taught" by a series of great revolutions and revolutionary movements of the masses. This is the method of deception, flattery, pretty phrases, innumerable promises, cheap sops, conceding the unimportant, retaining the important.

The peculiarity of the present moment in Russia consists in a dizzyingly rapid transition from the first method to the second, from violent oppression of the people to flattery and deceitful promises. Vaska the cat listens, but continues eating.† Miliukov and Guchkov hold power, protect the profits of capital, conduct an imperialist war in the interests of Russian and Anglo-French capital, while confining themselves to promises, declamation, impressive statements in reply to the speeches of "cooks" like Chkheidze, Tsereteli, Steklov, who threaten, exhort, conjure, beseech, demand, declare. . . . Vaska the cat listens, but continues eating.

But from day to day the trustful thoughtlessness and thoughtless trustfulness will dwindle away, especially among the proletarians and poorest peasants, whom life (their socio-economic position) teaches to distrust the capitalists.

The leaders of the petty bourgeoisie "must" teach the people to trust the bourgeoisie. The proletarians must teach the people to distrust it.

* From the Russian word *palka*, meaning stick, club.—*Ed.*
† Quotation from a fable by Krylov. The cook finds the cat eating chicken; the cook uses moral suasion. The cat listens but continues eating. Vaska is the Russian pet name for a tom cat.—*Ed.*

9. Revolutionary defencism must be recognised as the most imposing and striking manifestation of the petty-bourgeois wave which has overwhelmed "nearly everything." It is, indeed, the worst enemy of the further progress and success of the Russian Revolution.

Whoever has yielded on this point and has been unable to free himself is lost to the revolution. The masses, however, yield in a way different from that of the leaders, and they free themselves also differently, by another course of development, by other means.

Revolutionary defencism is, on the one hand, the result of the deception practiced on the masses by the bourgeoisie, the result of the peasants' and part of the workers' unthinking confidence; and on the other, the expression of the interests and standpoint of the petty proprietor, who to a certain extent is interested in annexations and bank profits, and who "religiously" guards the traditions of tsarism which demoralised the Great-Russians by doing hangman's work among other peoples.

The bourgeoisie deceives the people by playing upon the noble pride of the revolution and by painting the situation in a manner as if the socio-political character of the war, as far as Russia is concerned, has changed with the coming of this stage of the revolution, with the substitution of the bourgeois near-republic of Guchkov and Miliukov for the Tsar's monarchy. The people believe it,—for the time being—thanks, in a large degree, to the prejudices of old times, which cause them to see in the other peoples of Russia, outside of the Great-Russians, something like the property and the domain of the Great-Russians. The hideous demoralisation of the Great-Russian people by tsarism, which taught it to see in other peoples something inferior, something that "by right" belonged to Great-Russia, could not disappear at once.

It is required of us that we should be able to explain to the masses that the socio-political character of the war is determined not by the "good-will" of persons or groups, even peoples, but by the position of the class which conducts the war, by the class policy of which the war is a continuation, by the interrelations of capital as the dominant economic force in modern society, by the imperialist character of international capital by Russia's financial, banking, and diplomatic dependence upon England and France, etc. To explain this to the masses, skilfully and clearly, is not easy; none of us could do that all at once without errors.

But such, and only such, should be the trend or, rather, the contents of our propaganda. The slightest concession to revolutionary defencism is treason to Socialism, is a complete abandonment of internationalism, no matter what the beautiful phrases, what the "practical" considerations by which we may justify it.

The slogan, "Down with the War," is correct, to be sure, but it does not take into account the peculiarity of the tasks of the moment, the necessity to approach the masses in a different way. It reminds me of another slogan, "Down with the Tsar," with which an inexperienced agitator of the "good old days" went directly and simply to the village—to be beaten up. Those from the masses who are for revolutionary defencism are sincere, not in a personal, but in a class sense, *i. e.*, they belong to such classes (workers and poor peasants) as really gain nothing from annexations and the strangling of other peoples. They are quite different from the bourgeoisie and the intelligentsia who know very well that it is impossible to give up annexations without giving up the rule of capital, and who unscrupulously deceive the masses with beautiful phrases, with no end of promises, no end of assurances.

The average person who favours revolutionary defencism looks upon the thing in a simple matter-of-fact way: "I, for one, do not want any annexations, but the German 'presses' me hard, that means that I am defending a just cause and not any imperialist interests." To a man like this it must be explained very patiently that it is not a question of his personal wishes, but of mass, class, political relationships and conditions, of the connection between the war and the interests of capital, the war and the international network of banks, etc. Only such a struggle against defencism is serious and promises success, perhaps not very quick, but real and durable.

How the War Can Be Ended

10. The war cannot be ended "at will." It cannot be ended by the decision of one side. It cannot be ended by "sticking the bayonet into the ground," to use the expression of a soldier-defencist.

The war cannot be ended by an "agreement" between the Socialists of various countries, by "demonstrations" of the proletarians of various countries, by the "will" of the peoples, etc. All such phrases, filling the articles of the defencist, semi-defencist and semi-internationalist papers, as well as the numerous resolutions, appeals, manifestos, declarations of the Soviet of Workers' and Soldiers' Deputies, all these phrases are nothing but empty, harmless, goody-goody wishes of the petty-bourgeois. There is nothing more harmful than phrases like the "manifestation of the people's will to peace," the sequence of revolutionary proletarian actions (after the Russian proletariat comes the German), etc. All this is in the spirit of Louis Blanc, it is sweet dreams, a game of "political campaigning," in reality a repetition of the fable about Vaska the cat.

The war was not born out of the ill-will of capitalist robbers, although it undoubtedly is fought solely in their interests and they alone get rich from it. The war was born out of half a century of development of international capital, its billions of threads and connections. One cannot jump out of an imperialist war, one cannot attain a democratic unoppressive peace without overthrowing the power of capital, without the state power passing to a different class, the proletariat.

The Russian Revolution of March, 1917, was the beginning of the transformation of the imperialist war into civil war. The revolution took the first step towards ending the war. Only the second step can make the end of the war a certainty, namely, the passing of state power to the proletariat. This will be the beginning of a "breach in the front" on a world scale, a breach in the front of the interests of capital, and only after making this gap can the proletariat save mankind from the horrors of war and give it the blessings of a durable peace.

To such a "breach in the front" of capital the Russian Revolution has already brought the Russian proletariat by creating the Soviets of Workers' Deputies.

THE NEW TYPE OF STATE ARISING IN OUR REVOLUTION

11. The Soviets of Workers', Soldiers', Peasants', etc., Deputies are not understood, not only in the sense that their class character, their part in the Russian Revolution, is not clear to the majority. They are not understood also in the sense that they constitute a new form, rather, a new type of state.

The most perfect and advanced type of bourgeois state is that of a parliamentary democratic republic: power is vested in parliament; state machinery, apparatus, and organ of administration, are the usual ones: a standing army, police, bureaucracy, practically unchangeable, privileged, and standing above the people.

But revolutionary epochs, beginning with the end of the nineteenth century, bring to the fore the highest type of democratic state, the kind of state which in certain respects, to quote Engels, ceases to be a state, "is no state in the proper sense of the word." This is a state of the type of the Paris Commune, a state replacing the standing army and the police by a direct arming of the people itself. This is the essence of the Commune, which has been so much misrepresented and slandered by bourgeois writers, which, among other things, has been erroneously accused of wishing to "introduce" Socialism immediately.

This is the type of state which the Russian Revolution began to create in the years 1905 and 1917. A Republic of Soviets of Workers', Soldiers', Peasants', etc., Deputies, united in an all-Russian Constituent Assembly of the people's representatives, or in a Soviet of Soviets, etc.—this is what is already coming into life now, at this very time, upon the initiative of millions of people who, of their own accord, are creating a democracy in their own way, without waiting until Cadet gentlemen-professors will have written drafts of laws for a parliamentary bourgeois republic, or until the pedants and routine worshippers of petty-bourgeois "Social-Democracy," like Plekhanov and Kautsky, have abandoned their distortion of the teaching of Marxism concerning the state.

Marxism differs from Anarchism in that it admits the necessity of the state and state power in a revolutionary period in general, and in the epoch of transition from capitalism to Socialism in particular.

Marxism differs from the petty-bourgeois, opportunist "Social-Democracy" of Plekhanov, Kautsky and Co. in that it admits the necessity for the above-mentioned periods of a state not like the usual parliamentary bourgeois republic, but like the Paris Commune.

The main differences between the latter type of state and the bourgeois state are the following:

It is extremely easy to revert from a bourgeois republic to a monarchy (as history proves), since all the machinery of repression is left intact: army, police, bureaucracy. The Commune and the Soviets of Workers', Soldiers' and Peasants' Deputies smash and remove that machinery.

13

A parliamentary bourgeois republic strangles and crushes the independent political life of the masses, their direct participation in the democratic upbuilding of all state life from top to bottom. The opposite is true about the Soviets of Workers' and Soldiers' Deputies.

The latter reproduce the type of state that was being evolved by the Paris Commune and that Marx called the "finally discovered political form in which the economic liberation of the toilers can take place."

The usual objection is that the Russian people is not as yet prepared for the "introduction" of a Commune. This was the argument of serf owners who claimed that the peasants were not prepared for freedom. The Commune, *i. e.*, the Soviets of Workers' and Peasants' Deputies, does not "introduce," does not intend to "introduce" and should not introduce any reorganisations which are not absolutely ripe both in economic reality and in the consciousness of an overwhelming majority of the people. The more terrible the economic collapse and the crisis produced by the war, the more urgent is the need of a most perfect political form which facilitates the healing of the wounds inflicted by the war upon mankind. The less organisational experience the Russian people has, the more determinedly must we proceed with the organisational development of the people, not leaving it merely to the bourgeois politicians and bureaucrats with sinecures.

The sooner we cast off the pseudo-Marxian prejudices of Plekhanov, Kautsky and Co., the more diligently we start helping the people everywhere and immediately to organise Soviets of Workers' and Peasants' Deputies; the longer Messrs. Lvov and Co. procrastinate the convocation of the Constituent Assembly, the easier will it be for the people to make (through the medium of the Constituent Assembly, or outside of it, if Lvov delays its convocation long) its decision in favour of a Republic of Soviets of Workers' and Peasants' Deputies. Blunders in the new organisational reconstruction by the people are inevitable at the beginning, but it is better to blunder while progressing than to wait until the professors of law called by Mr. Lvov will have written laws concerning the convocation of the Constituent Assembly, the perpetuation of the parliamentary bourgeois republic and the strangulation of the Soviets of Workers' and Peasants' Deputies.

If we organise and conduct our propaganda efficiently, not only the proletarians but nine-tenths of the peasantry will be against the re-establishment of the police, against an irremovable and privileged bureaucracy, against an army separated from the people. This alone constitutes the new type of state.

12. The substitution of a national militia for the police is a transformation that follows from the entire course of the revolution and that is now being introduced in most localities of Russia. We must make it clear to the masses that in the majority of revolutions of the usual bourgeois type, a transformation of that sort was very ephemeral and that the bourgeoisie, however democratic and republican it may have been, soon re-established the police of the old tsarist type, a police separated from the people, commanded by bourgeois and capable of oppressing the people in every way.

There is only one way to prevent the re-establishment of the old police: to organise a national militia, to fuse it with the army (the standing army to be replaced by a general arming of the people). The militia should comprise all citizens of both sexes between the ages of fifteen and sixty-five, these age limits being selected approximately to exclude minors and old people. Capitalists should pay their employés, servants and others for the days devoted to public service in the militia. Unless women are drawn into taking an independent part not only in political life generally, but also in daily social service obligatory to every one, it is idle to speak not only of Socialism but even of complete and stable democracy. Certain "police" functions, such as the care of the sick, of the homeless children, pure food supervision, etc., will never be satisfactorily discharged until women are on a footing of perfect equality with men, not only on paper but in reality.

To prevent the re-establishment of the police, to attract all organisational forces of the entire people to the creation of a universal militia—such are the tasks that the proletariat must bring to the masses in order to protect, strengthen and develop the revolution.

The Agrarian and the National Programmes

13. We cannot know for certain at present whether a gigantic agrarian revolution will develop in the near future in the Russian village. We cannot know how deep is the class cleavage that has undoubtedly deepened in recent time between agricultural labourers and the poorest peasants ("semi-proletarians") on the one hand, and

the well-to-do and middle peasants (capitalists and petty capitalists) on the other. All such questions will be decided, and can be decided, by experience only.

We are in duty bound, however, as the party of the proletariat, immediately to step forth not only with an agrarian programme but also with the advocacy of immediately realisable practical measures in the interests of a peasant agrarian revolution in Russia.

We must demand the nationalisation of all lands, *i. e.*, the passing of all land ownership in the state to the central state power. This power shall fix the size, etc., of the migration fund,* issue laws for the conservation of forests, for melioration, etc., absolutely prohibit the intercession of middlemen between the landowner—the state—and the tenant—the tiller (prohibit every transfer of land). The disposition of all the land, however, the working out of all local rules of ownership and use, must not be left in the hands of bureaucrats and officials but be vested, wholly and exclusively, in the local and regional Soviets of Peasants' Deputies.

In order to improve the technique of grain raising and to increase production in general, in order also to develop rational cultivation on a large scale, socially controlled, we must see to it that every Peasants' Committee organises out of the various estates confiscated by it a large model estate controlled by the Soviets of Agricultural Labourers' Deputies.

To offset the petty-bourgeois phrases and policy of the Socialists-Revolutionists, particularly the empty words concerning the "standard of consumption" or "labour standard," the "socialisation of the land," etc., the party of the proletariat must make it clear that the system of small peasant households where production for the market prevails cannot save mankind from poverty or oppression.

Without necessarily splitting at once the Soviets of Peasants' Deputies, the party of the proletariat must make clear the necessity of organising special Soviets of Agricultural Labourers' Deputies and special Soviets of Deputies from the poorest (semi-proletarian) peasants or, at least, special conferences of Deputies of the same class position continually meeting as separate groups or parties within the Soviets of Peasants' Deputies. Otherwise all the sugary phraseology of the Narodniks on the subject of the peasants gen-

* Land to be allotted to peasants desirous of migrating from congested areas.—*Ed.*

erally will prove a shield to cover up the deception of the destitute mass by the well-to-do peasants who are only one of the varieties of capitalists.

To offset the bourgeois-liberal or purely bureaucratic preachments on the part of many Socialists-Revolutionists and Soviets of Workers' and Peasants' Deputies who advise the peasants not to seize the landlords' lands and not to start any agrarian reform pending the convocation of the Constituent Assembly, the party of the proletariat must urge the peasants to bring about at once, on their own initiative, the agrarian transformation, and to confiscate at once the landlords' lands by the decisions of the local Soviets of Peasants' Deputies.

In this connection, it is particularly important to insist on the necessity of increasing the production of foodstuffs for the soldiers at the front and for the cities, on the absolute inadmissibility of any kind of destruction or wastage of stock, tools, machinery, buildings, etc.

14. As regards the national question, the proletarian party must, first of all, insist on the promulgation and immediate realisation of full freedom of separation from Russia for all nations and peoples who were oppressed by tsarism, who were forcibly included or forcibly retained within the boundaries of the state, *i. e.*, annexed.

All statements, declarations and manifestoes concerning the renunciation of annexations not accompanied by actual realisation of the freedom of separation, reduce themselves to bourgeois deception of the people, or to petty-bourgeois pious wishes.

The proletarian party strives to create as large a state as possible, for this is in the interest of the workers; it strives to bring the nations closely together, to fuse them, but it intends to bring that about not by the use of force, but only by a free, brotherly union of the workers and the toiling masses of all nations.

The more democratic the Russian republic is, the more speedily it will organise itself into a republic of Soviets of Workers' and Peasants' Deputies, the more powerful the force of attraction such a republic will be for the toiling masses of all nations.

Full freedom of separation, the broadest possible local (and national) autonomy, guarantees for the rights of national minorities elaborated in detail—such is the programme of the revolutionary proletariat.

15. The party of the proletariat cannot by any means make it its aim to introduce Socialism in a country of small peasantry as long as the overwhelming majority of the population has not realised the necessity of a Socialist revolution.

Only bourgeois sophists, however, hiding behind "near-Marxist" phrases, can deduct from this truth a justification of a policy that tends to put off immediate revolutionary measures, which are perfectly ripe, which were frequently introduced during the war by a number of bourgeois states, and which are absolutely necessary for the struggle against approaching total economic disorganisation and famine.

Such measures as the nationalisation of the land, of all the banks and capitalist syndicates or, at least, the establishment of an immediate control of the Soviets of Workers' Deputies over them, by no means signifying the "introduction" of Socialism, must be absolutely fought for, and as far as possible introduced in a revolutionary way. Without such measures, which are only steps toward Socialism, and which are completely realisable economically, it is impossible to heal the wounds inflicted by the war and to prevent the threatening collapse. The party of the revolutionary proletariat will never hesitate to lay hands on the unheard-of profits of the capitalists and bankers who enrich themselves most scandalously "in the war."

THE STATE OF AFFAIRS IN THE SOCIALIST INTERNATIONAL

16. The international obligations of the Russian working class have been put in the forefront most forcibly these days.

Everybody swears by internationalism in our day; even chauvinist-defencists, even Messrs., Plekhanov and Potresov, even Kerensky, call themselves internationalists. The more urgent is the duty of the proletarian party to contrast, most clearly, decisively, definitely, internationalism in deed with internationalism in words.

Mcre appeals to the workers of all countries, empty professions of international faith, direct or indirect attempts to establish a "sequence" of proletarian action in the various belligerent countries, attempts at concluding "agreements" between the Socialists of the belligerent countries concerning revolutionary struggle,

pother about Socialist congresses aiming at peace propaganda,—
all this, as far as the objective meaning is concerned, no matter
how sincere the authors of such ideas, attempts and plans may be,
is mere talk, at best innocent little wishes good only to cover up the
deception of the masses by the chauvinists. The French social-
chauvinists, most adroit and best versed in methods of parliamentary juggling, have long since broken the record of spouting
incredibly loud and ringing pacifist and internationalist phrases
coupled with the most brazen betrayal of Socialism and the International, by entering governments that are waging an imperialist
war, by voting for credits or loans (as Chkheidze, Skobelev,
Tsereteli and Steklov have been doing recently in Russia) and
actively opposing the revolutionary struggle in their own country,
etc., etc.

Good people often forget the cruel, savage setting of the imperialist World War. In such a setting, phrases are intolerable;
innocent sweet wishes are despicable.

There is one, and only one, kind of real internationalism: hard
work at developing the revolutionary movement and the revolutionary struggle in one's own land, and the support (by propaganda,
sympathy, material aid) of such, and only such, struggles and
policies in every country without exception.

Everything else is deception and Manilovism.*

The international Socialist and labour movement the world over
has in the course of two and a half years of war evolved three
tendencies. Whoever declines to recognise the existence of these
three tendencies, to analyse them, to fight persistently for real active
internationalism, condemns himself to impotence, helplessness and
errors.

The three tendencies are:

1. Social-chauvinists, *i. e.*, Socialists in words and chauvinists
in fact, people who are for "national defence" in any imperialist
war (and particularly in this imperialist war).

These men are our class enemies. They have gone over to the
bourgeoisie.

Such is the majority among the official leaders of the official
Social-Democracy in every country. Plekhanov and Co. in Russia,
the Scheidemanns in Germany, Renaudel, Guesde and Sembat in

---

* Manilov is a character in Gogol's *Dead Souls* who is sentimental and
dreams of impossible things.—*Ed.*

19

France, Bissolati and Co. in Italy, Hyndman, the Fabians and the Labourites in England, Branting and Co. in Sweden, Troelstra and his party in Holland, Stauning and his party in Denmark, Victor Berger and other "defenders of the fatherland" in America, etc.

2. The second tendency, the so-called "centre," people vacillating between social-chauvinism and real internationalism.

Those of the "centre" swear and vow that they are Marxists, internationalists, that they are for peace, for exerting "pressure" upon the governments, for presenting all sorts of "demands" to the governments that the latter "manifest the people's will to peace," for all sorts of peace campaigns, for peace without annexations, etc., etc.,—and for peace with the social-chauvinists. The "centre" is for "unity," the "centre" is against schism.

The "centre" is a realm of sweet petty-bourgeois phrases, of internationalism in words, cowardly opportunism and fawning before the social-chauvinists in deeds.

The gist of the matter is that the members of the "centre" do not believe in the necessity of revolution against their bourgeois governments; do not preach such revolution; do not carry on any determined revolutionary struggles, but in order to dodge such struggles resort to trite and most "Marxist" sounding excuses.

The social-chauvinists are our class enemies, they are bourgeois elements in the labour movement. Objectively they represent strata or groups of the working class bribed by the bourgeoisie (better wages, positions of honour, etc.) and helping their bourgeoisie to rob and oppress small and weak peoples, to fight for the division of capitalist spoils.

The members of the "centre" group are routine worshippers, slaves of rotten legality, corrupted by parliamentarism, etc., bureaucrats accustomed to nice sinecures and "peaceful" labours. Historically and economically, they do not represent any special stratum of society; they only represent the transition from the earlier labour movement as it was between 1871 and 1914, from a period that had given much valuable experience to the proletariat particularly in the indispensable art of slow, continued, systematic organisation work on a large, very large, scale, to the new period which has become objectively necessary since the first imperialist World War which has inaugurated the era of social revolution.

In Karl Kautsky, the main leader and representative of the "centre" and the most outstanding authority in the Second International

(1889-1914), we have seen since August, 1914, a complete break-down of Marxism, an unheard-of lack of principles, a series of most pitiful vacillations and betrayals. Among these centrists are Kautsky, Haase, Ledebour, and the so-called "labour-group" [*Arbeitsgemeinschaft*] in the Reichstag; in France, Longuet, Pressemane and the so-called "*minoritaires*" (Mensheviks) in general; in England, Philip Snowden, Ramsay MacDonald and numerous other leaders of the Independent Labour Party, and a part of the British Socialist Party; Morris Hillquit and many others in the United States; Turati, Treves, Modigliani and others in Italy; Robert Grimm and others in Switzerland; Victor Adler and Co. in Austria; the party of the Organisation Committee, Axelrod, Martov, Chkheidze, Tsereteli and others in Russia, etc.

It goes without saying that at times individual persons do unconsciously drift from social-chauvinism to "centrism," and vice versa. Every Marxist knows, however, that classes retain their distinguishing characteristics regardless of the free movement of individuals from one class to another; similarly, movements in political life retain their distinguishing characteristics regardless of the free migration of individuals from one movement to another, and despite all attempts and efforts to fuse movements.

3. The third, real internationalist trend is most nearly represented by the "Zimmerwald Left." In the supplement we reprint its Manifesto of September, 1915, so that the reader may become acquainted with the inception of this movement.

It is characterised by the complete break with social-chauvinism and "centrism," a relentless war against the imperialist home government and the imperialist home bourgeoisie. Its principle is "Our greatest enemy is at home." A ruthless struggle against nauseatingly sweet social-pacifist phrases (a social-pacifist is a Socialist in words, and a bourgeois-pacifist in deeds; bourgeois-pacifists dream of an everlasting peace without the overthrow of the yoke and domination of capital) and against all sophistry employed to demonstrate the impossibility, the inappropriateness, the untimeliness of a proletarian revolutionary struggle, of a proletarian Socialist revolution in connection with the present war.

The most outstanding representative of this tendency in Germany is the "Spartacus" * or "International" Group, to which Karl Lieb-

* The group of revolutionary internationalists who later formed the Communist Party of Germany.—*Ed.*

21

knecht belongs. Karl Liebknecht is the best known representative of this tendency and of the *new*, real, proletarian International.

Karl Liebknecht called upon the workers and soldiers of Germany to turn their guns upon their own government. Karl Liebknecht did that openly from the tribune of parliament, the Reichstag. He then went out to a demonstration on Potsdamer Platz, one of the largest public squares in Berlin, distributing illegally printed proclamations carrying the slogan "Down with the government." He was arrested and sentenced to hard labour. He is now serving his term in a German prison, like hundreds, if not thousands, of other real German Socialists who have been imprisoned for waging a struggle against war.

Karl Liebknecht attacked mercilessly in his speeches and his writings not only the German Plekhanovs and the Potresovs (the Scheidemanns, Legiens, Davids, etc.), but also the German centrists, the German Chkheidzes and Tseretelis (Kautsky, Haase, Ledebour and Co.).

Karl Liebknecht and his friend, Otto Rühle, two out of one hundred and ten [Social-Democratic] Deputies in the Reichstag, broke the discipline, destroyed the "unity" with the "centre" and the chauvinists, and fought against everybody. Liebknecht alone represents Socialism, the proletarian cause, the proletarian revolution. The rest of the German Social-Democracy, to quote the apt words of Rosa Luxemburg (also a member and one of the leaders of the Spartacus group), is "a stinking corpse."

Another group of real internationalists in Germany is gathered around the Bremen paper, *Arbeiterpolitik*.

Closest to real internationalists are: in France, Loriot and his friends (Bourderon and Merrheim have degenerated into social-pacificism), as well as the Frenchman Henri Guilbeaux, who is publishing in Switzerland a paper called *Demain;* in England, the paper *Trade Unionist,* and some of the members of the British Socialist Party and of the Independent Labour Party (for instance, William Russell, who has openly called for a break with the leaders who have betrayed Socialism), the Scottish public school teacher and Socialist, MacLean, who has been sentenced to hard labour by the bourgeois government of England for his revolutionary activity against the war; hundreds of English Socialists who are in jail for the same offence. They, only they, are internationalists in deed. In the United States, the Socialist Labour

Party and certain elements of the opportunist Socialist Party which in January, 1917, began to publish the paper *The Internationalist;* in Holland, the party of the "Tribunists," those who publish the daily paper *Tribune* (Anton Pannekoek, Herman Gorter, Wynkoop, and Henriette Roland-Holst, who, though a centrist at Zimmerwald, has now joined our ranks); in Sweden, the party of the youth or the Left with leaders such as Lindhagen, Ture Nerman, Carlson, Ström and S. Höglund, who at Zimmerwald was personally active in the organisation of the Zimmerwald Left, and who is now serving a prison term for his activity against the war; in Denmark, Trier and his friends who have left the now purely bourgeois "Social-Democratic" Party, headed by Minister Stauning; in Bulgaria, the "narrow-minded";* in Italy, the closest are Constantino Lazzari, secretary of the party, and Serrati, editor of the central organ, Avanti; in Poland, Karl Radek, Hanecki and other leaders of the Social-Democracy, united through the "District Administration"; Rosa Luxemburg, Tyszka, and other leaders of the Social-Democracy united through the "Central Administration"; in Switzerland, those "Lefts," who wrote the supporting argument for the "referendum" (January, 1917), in order to fight against the social-chauvinists and the "centre" of their country and who at the Zürich Canton Socialist Convention, held at Töss on February 11, 1917, introduced a consistently revolutionary resolution against the war; in Austria, the young Left-wing friends of Friedrich Adler, who have been acting partly through the "Karl Marx" Club, at Vienna, a club now closed by the very reactionary Austrian government which is destroying Adler for his heroic but ill-considered attempt upon the life of the Prime Minister, etc., etc.

It is not a matter of shadings, these exist even among the "Lefts." It is a matter of the entire tendency. The point is, that it is by no means easy to be an internationalist in deeds during a terrible imperialist war. Such people are rare, but it is on them alone that the future of Socialism depends; they alone are the leaders of the masses, not the corrupters of the masses.

The difference between reformists and revolutionists in the ranks of the Social-Democrats and Socialists in general cannot but undergo, objectively, a positive change in the midst of an imperialist war. He who simply confines himself to "demanding" from bourgeois

* The revolutionary internationalist wing of the Bulgarian Social-Democracy. —*Ed.*

governments "the conclusion of peace" or "the manifestation of the will of the peoples toward peace," etc., is, in fact, degenerating into a reformist. For, objectively, the problem of war can be solved only in a revolutionary way.

There is no escape from this war to a democratic, non-oppressive peace, to a liberation of the peoples from the yoke of paying billions of interest to the capitalists enriched by the war, there is no other escape except a proletarian revolution.

We can, and we must, demand all sorts of reforms from the bourgeois governments, but it is impossible, without falling into Manilovism and reformism, to demand from those people and classes who are entangled by a thousand ties of imperialist capital to break those ties; yet unless we break those ties all talk of war against war is empty, deceitful prattle.

The "Kautskians," the "centre," are revolutionists in words, reformists in deeds, internationalists in words, supporters of social-chauvinism in deeds.

THE BREAKDOWN OF THE ZIMMERWALD INTERNATIONAL. THE NECESSITY OF FORMING A THIRD INTERNATIONAL

17. The Zimmerwald International took from the very first a vacillating, Kautskian, "centrist" position which immediately compelled the Zimmerwald Left to fence itself off, to separate itself from the rest, and to come forth with its own Manifesto (published in Switzerland in Russian, in German and in French).

The chief fault of the Zimmerwald International, the cause of its breakdown (for from a political and ideological viewpoint it has already broken down), was its vacillation, its indecision, when it came to the most important practical and all-determining question of breaking completely with the social-chauvinists and the old social-chauvinist International, headed by Vandervelde and Huysmans at The Hague (Holland), etc.

We Russians do not as yet know that the Zimmerwald majority are really Kautskians. But this is a basic fact which must not be minimised and of which Western Europe is now fully aware. Even that chauvinist, that extreme German chauvinist, Heilmann, editor of the arch-chauvinist *Chemnitzer Volksstimme* and contributor to the arch-chauvinist *Glocke* of Parvus (a "Social Democrat," of course, and an ardent partisan of the Social-Democratic "unity"), was compelled to acknowledge in the press that the "centre," or Kautskyism, and the Zimmerwald majority were one and the same thing.

The end of 1916 and the beginning of 1917 had definitely proved it. In spite of the condemnation of social-pacifism contained in the Kienthal Manifesto,* the whole Zimmerwald Right, the entire Zimmerwald majority, degenerated into social-pacifism: Kautsky and Co., in a series of declarations during the months of January and February, 1917; Bourderon and Merrheim in France, who cast their votes together with the social-chauvinists for the pacifist resolutions of the Socialist Party (December, 1916) and of the *Confédération Generale du Travail* (the national organisation of French labour unions), also in December, 1916; Turati and Co. in Italy, where the entire party took a social-pacifist position, while Turati himself, in a speech delivered on December 17, 1916, "slipped" (and not by accident, of course) into nationalistic phrases embellishing the imperialist war.

In January, 1917, the chairman of the Zimmerwald and Kienthal conferences, Robert Grimm, joined hands with the social-chauvinists of his own party (Greulich, Pflueger, Gustav Mueller and others) against the real internationalists.

At two conferences of Zimmerwaldists of various countries, held in January and February of 1917, this dual, double-faced behaviour of the Zimmerwald majority was formally stigmatised by the Left internationalists of several countries, by Münzenberg, secretary of the internationalist organisation of the Young People's [Socialist] movement and editor of the excellent internationalist publication *Die Jugendinternationale,* by Zinoviev, representative of the Central Committee of our party, by Karl Radek of the Polish Social-Democratic Party (the "District Administration"), by Hartstein, a German Social-Democrat and member of the "Spartacus Group."

To the Russian proletariat much has been given. Nowhere on earth has the working class yet succedeed in unfolding so much revolutionary energy as it has in Russia. But much is demanded from those to whom much is given.

We can stand no longer this Zimmerwald mire. We must not, on account of the Zimmerwald "Kautskians," remain more or less allied with the chauvinist International of the Plekhanovs and

---

* The Manifesto of the Conference held at Kienthal, Switzerland, in 1916 of internationalist groups dominated by Centrists.—*Ed.*

25

Scheidemanns. We must break with this International immediately. We ought to remain in Zimmerwald only to gather information.

It is precisely we who must found, right now, without delay, a new, revolutionary, proletarian International, or rather, not to fear to acknowledge publicly that this new International is already established and working.

This is the International of those "internationalists in deed," whom I have fully enumerated above, they alone represent the revolutionary, internationalist masses, they and not the corrupters of the masses.

Even if there are few Socialists of that type, let every Russian worker ask himself how many really conscious revolutionists there were in Russia on the eve of the March Revolution in 1917.

It is not so much a question of numbers; it is a question of expressing correctly the ideas and the policy of the truly revolutionary proletariat. Never mind about "proclaiming" internationalism; the essential thing is for us to be, even when the times are most trying, real internationalists in deed.

Let us not deceive ourselves by hopes for agreements and international congresses. As long as this imperialist war lasts, international relations are held as in a vise by the military dictatorship of the imperialist bourgeoisie. If even the "republican" Miliukov who had to suffer the "parallel government" of the Soviet of Workers' Deputies, did not allow into Russia, in April, 1917, Fritz Platten, the Swiss Socialist, secretary of the party and internationalist, member of the Zimmerwald and Kienthal conferences, although Platten was married to a Russian woman, and was going for a visit to his wife's relatives, and although he had taken part in the Revolution of 1905 in Riga, had served a term in a Russian prison for that offence, had given bail to the tsarist government for his release and wanted that bail returned to him—if the republican Miliukov could do such a thing, in April, 1917, and in Russia, then we can see how much stock we may take in the promises and offers, phrases and declarations made by the bourgeoisie on the subject of peace without annexations, etc.

And how about the arrest of Trotsky by the English Government? And how about Martov being refused permission to leave Switzerland; how about the attempt made to lure him to England, where he would share Trotsky's fate?

Let us not create illusions for ourselves. We need no self-deception.

"To wait" for international conferences and congresses is simply to betray internationalism, since it is established that Socialists loyal to internationalism are not allowed to come here even from Stockholm, they are not allowed even to send letters to us, despite the thoroughly rigorous military censorship that can be and is fully exercised on all writings.

Let us not "wait," let rather our party found at once a third International, and hundreds of Socialists imprisoned in England and in Germany will heave a sigh of relief; thousands upon thousands of German workers who are now organising strikes and demonstrations in an effort to frighten the scoundrel and murderer, Wilhelm, will read in illegal leaflets about our decision, about our fraternal confidence in Karl Liebknecht (and in him alone), about the decision to fight even now the "revolutionary defencists"; they will read and gain strength in their revolutionary internationalism.

Much is demanded from him to whom much is given. There is no other land on earth as free as Russia is now. Let us make use of this freedom not to support the bourgeoisie or bourgeois "revolutionary defencism," but to organise a third International, bold and honest and proletarian, the kind which Liebknecht would have, an International which will set its face boldly against all traitors, all social-chauvinists and the vacillating people of the "centre."

18. After what I have just said, I need not waste any words to explain that a union of the Social-Democrats of Russia is impossible.

Rather stay alone, as Liebknecht did, that is, remain with the revolutionary proletariat, than to entertain even for a minute any thought of a union with the party of the Organisation Committee, with Chkheidze and Tsereteli, who have joined hands with Potresov of the *Rabochaia Gazeta,* who voted for the war loan in the Executive Committee of the Soviet of Workers' Deputies, and who have degenerated into "revolutionary defencism."

Let the dead bury their dead.

Whosoever wants to help vacillating souls, should first stop vacillating himself.

A NAME FOR OUR PARTY WHICH WOULD BE SCIENTIFICALLY SOUND AND CONDUCIVE TO PROLETARIAN CLASS THINKING

19. I am coming to the last point, the name of our party. We must call ourselves the Communist Party—just as Marx and Engels called themselves Communists.

We must insist that we are Marxists and that we have as a basis the *Communist Manifesto*, which has been perverted and betrayed by the Social-Democracy on two important points: (1) The workers have no country; "national defence" in an imperialist war is a betrayal of Socialism; (2) Marx's teaching about the state has been perverted by the Second International.

The term "Social-Democracy" is unscientific, as Marx showed repeatedly, particularly in the *Critique of the Gotha Programme*, in 1875, and as Engels restated in a more popular form, in 1894. Mankind can pass directly from capitalism only into Socialism, *i. e.,* into social ownership of the means of production and the distribution of products according to the work of the individual. Our party looks farther ahead than that: Socialism is bound sooner or later to ripen into Communism, whose banner bears the motto: "From each according to his ability, to each according to his needs."

That is the first reason.

Here is my second: The second part of the term "Social-*Democracy*" is scientifically wrong. Democracy is only a form of state, while we Marxists are opposed to every form of state.

The leaders of the Second International (1889-1914), Messrs. Plekhanov, Kautsky and their ilk, perverted and debased Marxism.

The difference between Marxism and Anarchism is that Marxism admits the necessity of the state during the transition from capitalism to Socialism; but (and here is where we differ from Kautsky and Co.) not the kind of state found in the usual, parliamentary, bourgeois, democratic republic, but rather something like the Paris Commune of 1871 and the Soviets of Workers' Deputies of 1905 and 1917.

There is a third reason: Life and the revolution have already established here in a concrete way (although in a form which is still weak and embryonic), this new type of "state," though it is not really a state in the proper sense of the word.

It is now a question of the action of the masses and not merely of theories of leaders.

Essentially the state is the power exercised over the masses by a group of armed men separated from the people.

Our new state, which is now in process of being born, is also a real state, for we, too, need detachments of armed men; we, too, need the strictest order, and the ruthless crushing of all attempts at a tsarist as well as a Guchkov-bourgeois counter-revolution.

But our forming, new state is not yet a state in the proper sense of the word, for the detachments of armed men found in many parts of Russia are really the masses themselves, the people, and not simply privileged individuals, practically unremovable, placed above and separated from the people.

We ought to look forward, not backward; we ought to look away from the usual bourgeois type of democracy which has been strengthening the domination of the bourgeoisie by means of the old, monarchistic organs of government,—the police, the army, and the bureaucracy.

We must look forward to the advent of the newly born democracy, which is already ceasing to be a democracy, for democracy means the people's rule, while, obviously, an armed people could not rule over itself.

The word democracy is not only not scientific when applied to the Communist Party, but, since March, 1917, it has simply become a blinker placed upon the eyes of the revolutionary people, preventing the latter from establishing boldly, freely, and on its own initiative a new form of power: the Soviets of Workers', Soldiers', etc., Deputies, as the sole power in the state and as the harbinger of the "withering away" of the state as such.

There is a fourth reason: We must take into account the objective international condition of Socialism.

Its condition is no longer what it was between the years 1871 and 1914, when Marx and Engels consciously allowed the inaccurate, opportunist term "Social-Democracy." For history proved that what was most needed in those days, *i. e.*, right after the defeat of the Paris Commune, was slow work of organisation and enlightenment. Nothing else was possible. The Anarchists were then, as they are now, theoretically, economically, and politically wrong. The Anarchists made a wrong estimate of the time, for they did not understand the world situation: the worker of England corrupted by imperialist profits; the Paris Commune destroyed; the bourgeois-national movement in Germany flushed with recent victory; and semi-feudal Russia still sleeping the sleep of centuries.

Marx and Engels gauged the hour accurately; they understood the international situation; they realised the need of a slow approach toward the beginning of the Social Revolution.

We, in turn, must understand the peculiarities and the tasks of the new epoch. Let us not imitate the woe-Marxians of whom Marx himself said: "I sowed dragons and I reaped fleas." *

The objective needs of capitalism which has grown into imperialism have brought forth the imperialist war. This war has brought mankind to the brink of a precipice, to the destruction of civilisation, the ruin and brutalisation of countless millions of human beings.

There is no other way out, except a proletarian revolution.

And just when that revolution is beginning, when it is taking its first awkward, timid, weak, unconscious steps, when it is still trusting the bourgeoisie, at that moment the majority (it is the truth, it is a fact) of the Social-Democratic leaders, of the Social-Democratic parliamentarians, of the Social-Democratic papers, in a word, all those who could spur the masses to action, or at least the majority of them, are betraying Socialism, are selling Socialism, are going to fight the battles of their national bourgeoisie.

The masses are distracted, baffled, deceived by their leaders.

And should we aid and abet that deception by retaining the old and worn-out party name, which is as decayed as the Second International?

It may be that many workers understand the meaning of Social-Democracy honestly. It is high time that we learn to distinguish between the objective and the subjective.

Subjectively, these workers, who are Social-Democrats, are the most loyal leaders of the proletarian masses.

Objectively, however, the world situation is such that the old name of our party helps to fool the masses and retard their onward march. Every day, in every paper, in every parliamentary group, the masses see leaders, *i. e.*, people whose voice carries far, whose acts are very much in evidence, who also call themselves Social-Democrats, who are "for unity" with the betrayers of

* An expression which Marx borrowed from Heine.—*Ed.*

Socialism, the social-chauvinists, and who are trying to collect on the notes issued by Social-Democracy. . . .

Are there any reasons against the new name? We are told that one may confuse us with Anarchists-Communists.

Why are we not afraid of being confused with the Social-Nationalists, the Social-Liberals, the Radical-Socialists, the foremost, the most adroit bourgeois party in the French Republic at deceiving the masses? We are told: "The masses have grown used to the name, the workers have learned to love their Social-Democratic Party."

That is the only reason, but this reason goes counter to the teachings of Marxism, disregards the revolutionary tasks of to-morrow, the objective position of Socialism the world over, the shameful breakdown of the Second International, and the injury done to the cause by the pack of "also Social-Democrats" surrounding the proletarians.

This reason is based solely on laziness, somnolence, and love of routine.

We want to rebuild the world. We want to end this imperialist World War in which hundreds of millions of people are involved and billions of dollars are invested, a war which cannot be ended in a truly democratic way without the greatest proletarian revolution in history.

And here we are, afraid of our own shadow. Here we are, keeping on our backs the same old soiled shirt. . . .

It is high time to cast off the soiled shirt, it is high time to put on clean linen.

N. Lenin.

Petrograd, April 23, 1917.
First published as a separate pamphlet, September, 1917, by the "Priboi" publishing firm.

ON THE TASKS OF THE PROLETARIAT IN THE PRESENT REVOLUTION

As I only arrived in Petrograd on the night of April 16, I could, of course, only on my own responsibility and admittedly without sufficient preparation render a report on April 17 on the problems of the revolutionary proletariat.

The only thing I could do to facilitate matters for myself and for honest opponents was to prepare written theses. I read them, and gave the text to Comrade Tsereteli. I read them twice, very slowly: First at the meeting of the Bolsheviks, then at the joint meeting of Bolsheviks and Mensheviks.

I am publishing these personal theses, provided with very short explanatory notes, which were developed in more detail in the report:

THESES

1. In our attitude toward the war not the smallest concession must be made to "revolutionary defencism," for under the new government of Lvov and Co., owing to the capitalist nature of this government, the war on Russia's part remains a predatory imperialist war.

The class-conscious proletariat may give its consent to a revolutionary war, actually justifying revolutionary defencism, only on condition (a) that all power be transferred to the proletariat and its ally, the poorest section of the peasantry; (b) that all annexations be renounced in deeds, not merely in words; (c) that there be a complete break, in practice, with all interests of capital.

In view of the undoubted honesty of the mass of rank and file representatives of revolutionary defencism who accept the war only as a necessity and not as a means of conquest, in view of their being deceived by the bourgeoisie, it is necessary most thoroughly, persistently, patiently to explain to them their error, to explain the inseparable connection between capital and the imperialist war, to prove that without the overthrow of capital, it is *impossible* to conclude the war with a really democratic, non-oppressive peace.

This view is to be widely propagated among the army units in the field.

Fraternisation.

2. The peculiarity of the present situation in Russia is that it represents a *transition* from the first stage of the revolution, which, because of the inadequate organisation and insufficient class-consciousness of the proletariat, led to the assumption of power by the bourgeoisie—to its second stage which is to place power in the hands of the proletariat and the poorest strata of the peasantry.

This transition is characterised, on the one hand, by a maximum of legality (Russia is now the freest of all the belligerent countries of the world); on the other, by the absence of oppression of the masses, and, finally, by the trustingly ignorant attitude of the masses toward the capitalist government, the worst enemy of peace and Socialism.

This peculiar situation demands of us an ability to adapt ourselves to specific conditions of party work amidst vast masses of the proletariat just awakened to political life.

3. No support to the Provisional Government; exposure of the utter falsity of all its promises, particularly those relating to the renunciation of annexations. Unmasking, instead of admitting, the illusion-breeding "demand" that *this* government, a government of capitalists, cease being imperialistic.

4. Recognition of the fact that in most of the Soviets of Workers' Deputies our party constitutes a minority, and a small one at that, in the face of the *bloc* of all the petty-bourgeois opportunist elements from the People's Socialists, the Socialists-Revolutionists down to the Organisation Committee (Chkheidze, Tsereteli, etc., Steklov, etc., etc.) who have yielded to the influence of the bourgeoisie and have been extending this influence to the proletariat as well.

It must be explained to the masses that the Soviet of Workers' Deputies is the only possible form of revolutionary government and, therefore, our task is, while this government is submitting to the influence of the bourgeoisie, to present a patient, systematic, and persistent analysis of its errors and tactics, an analysis especially adapted to the practical needs of the masses.

While we are in the minority, we carry on the work of criticism and of exposing errors, advocating all along the necessity of transferring the entire power of state to the Soviets of Workers' Deputies, so that the masses might learn from experience how to rid themselves of errors.

5. Not a parliamentary republic—a return to it from the Soviet of Workers' Deputies would be a step backward—but a republic of Soviets of Workers', Agricultural Labourers' and Peasants' Deputies, throughout the land, from top to bottom.

Abolition of the police, the army, the bureaucracy.*

All officers to be elected and to be subject to recall at any time, their salaries not to exceed the average wage of a competent worker.

6. In the agrarian programme, the emphasis must be shifted to the Soviets of Agricultural Labourers' Deputies.

Confiscation of all private lands.

Nationalisation of all lands in the country, and management of such lands by local Soviets of Agricultural Labourers' and Peasants' Deputies. A separate organisation of Soviets of Deputies of the poorest peasants. Creation of model agricultural establishments out of large estates (from 100 to 300 desiatinas, in accordance with local and other conditions and with the estimates of local institutions) under the control of the Soviet of Agricultural Labourers' Deputies, and at public expense.

7. Immediate merger of all the banks in the country into one general national bank, over which the Soviet of Workers' Deputies should have control.

8. Not the "introduction" of Socialism as an immediate task, but the immediate placing of the Soviet of Workers' Deputies in control of social production and distribution of goods.

9. Party tasks:

A. Immediate calling of a party convention.

B. Changing the party programme, mainly:

(1) Concerning imperialism and the imperialist war.

(2) Concerning our attitude toward the state and our demand for a "commune state." †

(3) Amending our antiquated minimum programme.

C. Changing the name of the party.‡

10. Rebuilding the International.

Taking the initiative in the creation of a revolutionary Inter-

* Substituting for the standing army the universal arming of the people.

† A state the model for which was given by the Paris Commune.

‡ Instead of "Social-Democracy," whose official leaders throughout the world have betrayed Socialism by going over to the bourgeoisie (defencists and vacillating Kautskians), we must call ourselves the *Communist Party*.

national, an International against the social-chauvinists and against the "centre." *

In order that the reader may understand why I was compelled especially to emphasise, as a rare exception, the "case" of a conscientious opponent, I would ask him to compare the above theses with the following objection of Mr. Goldenberg: Lenin, he said, "has planted the banner of civil war in the midst of revolutionary democracy" (quoted in Mr. Plekhanov's *Yedinstvo*, No. 5).

Is this not a gem?

I write, read, and ruminate:

"In view of the undoubted honesty of the mass of rank and file representatives of 'revolutionary defencism' who accept the war only as a necessity and not as a means of conquest, in view of their being deceived by the bourgeoisie, it is necessary most thoroughly, persistently, patiently to explain to them their error."

The gentlemen of the bourgeoisie, however, who call themselves Social-Democrats, who belong neither to the masses nor to the rank and file representatives of defencism, have the insolence to present my views in such words: "Has planted (!) the banner (!) of civil war (of which there is not a word in the theses nor in my speech) in the midst (!!) of revolutionary democracy. . . ."

What is it? How does this differ from pogrom propaganda? From the *Russkaia Volia?*

I write, read, and ruminate:

"The Soviet of Workers' Deputies is the only possible form of revolutionary government, and therefore, our task is . . . to present a patient, systematic, and persistent analysis of its errors and tactics, an analysis especially adapted to the practical needs of the masses."

But opponents of a certain calibre present my views as a call to "civil war in the midst of revolutionary democracy"!!

I attacked the Provisional Government because it has not fixed a date for convoking the Constituent Assembly either in the near future or at any time at all, confining itself to vague promises. I proved that without the Soviets of Workers' and Soldiers' Deputies,

* The "centre" in the international Social-Democracy is the tendency vacillating between chauvinists ("defencists") and internationalists, *i. e.,* Kautsky and Co. in Germany, Longuet and Co. in France, Chkheidze and Co. in Russia, Turati and Co. in Italy, MacDonald and Co. in England, etc.

the convocation of the Constituent Assembly is not guaranteed and its success impossible.

A view is attributed to me that I am opposed to the speediest convocation of the Constituent Assembly!!!

I would call these expressions "delirious," had not dozens of years of political fighting taught me to regard honesty in opponents as a rare exception.

In his paper Mr. Plekhanov called my speech "delirious." Very good, Mr. Plekhanov! But how awkward, uncouth, and slow-witted you are in your polemics! If I talked delirious stuff for two whole hours, why did an audience of hundreds tolerate this "delirium"? Further, why does your paper devote a whole column to reproducing this "delirium"? You have indeed made a bad shot in this matter!

It is, of course, much easier to shout, to scold, to rave than to make an attempt to relate, to explain, to recall how Marx and Engels in 1871, 1872, and 1875 viewed the experience of the Paris Commune and the kind of state the proletariat needs.

The former Marxist, Mr. Plekhanov, probably does not wish to think about Marxism.

I quoted the words of Rosa Luxemburg, who, on August 4, 1914, called the *German* Social-Democracy a "stinking corpse." Messrs. Plekhanov, Goldenberg and Co., however, feel "offended" . . . for whom?—for the German chauvinists who have been called chauvinists!

They have lost their way, these poor Russian social-chauvinists, Socialists in words and chauvinists in deeds.

N. LENIN.

Pravda, No. 26, April 20, 1917.

LETTERS ON TACTICS

FOREWORD

ON April 17, 1917, I was called upon to report on the subject indicated in the title, first, at a meeting of Bolsheviks in Petrograd. These were delegates to the All-Russian Conference of Workers' and Soldiers' Soviets, who had to leave for their homes and could not allow me to postpone it. At the close of the meeting, the chairman, Comrade G. Zinoviev, suggested in the name of the whole assembly that I repeat my report at the joint meeting of Bolshevik and Menshevik delegates, who wished to consider the question of unifying the Russian Social-Democratic Labour Party.

Difficult though it was for me immediately to repeat my report, I felt that I had no right to decline once it was demanded by comrades of my persuasion as well as by the Mensheviks, who, because of their impending departure, really could not grant me a respite.

In giving my report, I read the theses which were published in No. 26 of the *Pravda*, on April 20.*

Both the theses and my report created discord among the Bolsheviks themselves and the staff of the *Pravda*. After a number of consultations, we unanimously concluded that it would be expedient openly to discuss our differences, thus providing material for the All-Russian Conference of our party (the Russian Social-Democratic Labour Party, united under the Central Committee) which is to meet in Petrograd on May 3.

Complying with this decision concerning a discussion, I am publishing the following letters in which I do not pretend to have made an exhaustive study of the question, but wish only to outline the principal arguments, especially those essential for the *practical* tasks of the working-class movement.

AN ESTIMATE OF THE PRESENT SITUATION

Marxism demands of us a most exact, an objectively verifiable analysis of the interrelations of classes and of the concrete peculi-

* See pp. 32-36.—*Ed.*

liarities of each historic moment. We Bolsheviks have always tried to be true to this demand, which is absolutely imperative from the standpoint of giving a scientific foundation to politics.

"Our doctrine is not a dogma, but a guide to action," said Marx and Engels, who always scorned the mere acquisition and repetition of "formulæ," capable at best only of outlining *general* tasks, which are necessarily changed by the concrete economic and political circumstances of each particular period in the historical process.

What, then, are the clearly established objective facts by which the party of the revolutionary proletariat must be guided now in defining the tasks and forms of its activity?

In my first "Letter from Afar" ("The First Stage of the First Revolution") which was published in Nos. 14 and 15 of the *Pravda*, April 3 and 4, 1917,* and in my theses, I define the "peculiarity of the present moment" in Russia as a period of transition from the first stage of the revolution to the second. I therefore considered the basic slogan, the "order of the day" at that time to be: "Workers, you have displayed marvels of proletarian and popular heroism in the civil war against tsarism; you must display marvels of proletarian and nation-wide organisation in order to prepare your victory in the second stage of the revolution" (*Pravda*, No. 15).

What, then, is the first stage?

It is the passing of state power to the bourgeoisie.

Before the March revolution of 1917, state power in Russia was in the hands of one old class, namely, the feudal noble landlord class, headed by Nicholas Romanov.

After that revolution, state power is in the hands of another class, a new one, namely, the *bourgeoisie*.

The passing of state power from one class to another is the first, the main, the basic principle of a revolution, both in the strictly scientific and in the practical political meaning of that term.

To that extent, the bourgeois, or the bourgeois-democratic, revolution in Russia is *completed*.

But at this point we hear the noise of objectors, who readily call themselves "old Bolsheviks": Haven't we always maintained, they say, that a bourgeois-democratic revolution is culminated only in a "revolutionary dictatorship of the proletariat and the peasantry"? Is the agrarian revolution, which is a phase of the bourgeois-demo-

* See V. I. Lenin, *Letters from Afar*, Little Lenin Library, Vol. 8.—*Ed.*

cratic revolution, completed? On the contrary, is it not a fact that it has not yet begun?

My answer is: The Bolshevik slogans and ideas have been generally confirmed by history; but as to the concrete situation, things have turned out to be different, more original, more unique, more multicoloured than could have been anticipated by any one.

To ignore, to forget, this fact would mean to resemble those "old Bolsheviks" who more than once have played a sorry part in the history of our party when they repeated a formula, once acquired, without thinking, instead of studying the peculiarities of new living reality.

"The revolutionary-democratic dictatorship of the proletariat and the peasantry" has already become a reality* in the Russian Revolution, for this "formula" foresees only the interrrelation of classes, but it does not foresee the concrete political institutions which realise this interrelation, this co-operation. "The Soviet of Workers' and Soldiers' Deputies"—here you have "revolutionary-democratic dictatorship of the proletariat and peasantry" already realised in life.

This formula has become antiquated. Life brought it out of the realm of formulæ into the realm of reality, clothed it with flesh and blood, concretised it and thus changed it.

There is a new, a different task before us now: the split *within* this dictatorship between the proletarian elements (the anti-defencist, internationalist, "communist" elements who stand for the transition to the commune) and the petty-proprietor or petty-bourgeois elements (Chkheidze, Tsereteli, Steklov, the Socialists-Revolutionists and other revolutionary defencists, opponents of the movement toward the commune, adherents of "supporting" the bourgeoisie and the bourgeois government).

He who *now* speaks of "revolutionary-democratic dictatorship of the proletariat and peasantry" only, is behind the times, is therefore in practice on the side of the petty bourgeoisie and against the proletarian class struggle; such a one should be placed in the archive of "Bolshevik" pre-revolutionary antiques (it may be called the archive of "old Bolsheviks").

Revolutionary-democratic dictatorship of the proletariat and peasantry has already been realised, but in a very original way, with a number of extremely important modifications. I will deal with

---

* In a certain form and to a certain extent.

them separately, in one of the forthcoming letters. Now, however, it is necessary to acquire that incontestable truth that a Marxist must take cognisance of living life, of the true facts of reality, that he must not continue clinging to the theory of yesterday, which, like every theory, at best only outlines the main and the general, only approximately embracing the complexity of life.

"Theory, my friend, is grey, but green is the eternal tree of life."

Whoever questions the "completeness" of the bourgeois revolution from the old viewpoint, sacrifices living Marxism to a dead letter.

According to the old conception, the rule of the proletariat and peasantry, their dictatorship, can and must follow the rule of the bourgeoisie.

In real life, however, things have already turned out otherwise; an extremely original, new, unprecedented interlocking of one and the other has taken place. Side by side, together and simultaneously, we have both the rule of the bourgeoisie (the government of Lvov and Guchkov) and the revolutionary-democratic dictatorship of the proletariat and the peasantry, which *voluntarily* cedes power to the bourgeoisie and voluntarily makes itself an appendage of the bourgeoisie.

For it must not be forgotten that in Petrograd the power is actually in the hands of the workers and soldiers; the new government does not use violence against them, and cannot do so, because there is no police, there is no army separated from the people, there is no all-powerful officialdom placed above the people. This is a fact. It is the kind of fact that characterises a state of the type of the Paris Commune. This fact does not fit into the old framework of thought. One ought to be able to adapt the framework to life, rather than repeat the new senseless words about "dictatorship of the proletariat and the peasantry" *in general*.

Let us approach the question from another angle, in order to throw more light on it.

A Marxist must not leave the firm ground of the analysis of class relations. Power is in the hands of the bourgeoisie. But how about the mass of the peasants? Does it not *also* form a bourgeoisie, only of a different social stratum, of a different kind, of a different character? Wherefrom does it follow that *this* stratum cannot come into power, thus "completing" the bourgeois-democratic revolution? Why should this be impossible?

This is how the old Bolsheviks often argue.

My reply is that it is fully possible. But, in analysing a given situation, a Marxist must proceed not from the possible, but from the real.

Reality, however, shows us that the freely elected Soldiers' and Peasants' Deputies freely enter the second, the parallel government, freely supplementing, developing and completing it. And just as freely do they *give away* their power to the bourgeoisie, which phenomenon does not in the least "undermine" the theory of Marxism, for we have always known and have repeatedly pointed out that the bourgeoisie maintains itself not only by force but also by the lack of class-consciousness, the clinging to old habits, the timidity, the lack of organisation on the part of the masses.

Now, in the face of this reality of to-day, it would be simply ridiculous to turn away from the fact and to speak of "possibilities."

It is possible that the peasantry might seize all the land and all the power. Not only do I not forget this possibility, not only do I not confine myself to the present, but I definitely and clearly formulate the agrarian programme considering the new phenomenon, *i. e.*, the deep chasm between the agricultural labourers and the poorest peasants on the one hand and the peasant landowners on the other hand.

Something else is possible, however; it is possible that the peasants will listen to the advice of the petty-bourgeois party of the Socialists-Revolutionists that has yielded to the influence of the bourgeoisie, that has gone over to defencism and that advises waiting for the Constituent Assembly, although not even the date of its convocation has so far been set.*

It is possible that the peasants will adhere to and prolong their pact with the bourgeoisie, which they have concluded now through the medium of the Soviets of Workers' and Soldiers' Deputies, not only in form, but in deed.

Many things are possible. It would be the greatest mistake were we to forget the agrarian movement and the agrarian programme. But it would be equally wrong to forget the reality which shows us the fact of an agreement—or, to use a more exact, less legal, and

---

* Lest my words be misinterpreted, I will anticipate at once: I am absolutely in favour of the Soviets of Agricultural Labourers and Peasants immediately taking possession of all the land, on condition that they themselves should preserve the strictest order and discipline, not permitting the least injury to machines, buildings, and live stock, in no way disorganising agriculture and the production of bread stuffs, but increasing them, for the soldiers need twice as much bread, and the people must not starve.

more economic, class expression—the fact of *class collaboration* between the bourgeoisie and the peasantry.

When this fact ceases to be a fact, when the peasantry has separated itself from the bourgeoisie, when it has seized the land and power against the bourgeoisie—then there will be a new stage of the bourgeois-democratic revolution; and of that it will be necessary to speak separately.

A Marxist who, in view of the possibility of such a future stage, were to forget his duty at the present time when the peasantry is in agreement with the bourgeoisie, would turn petty-bourgeois. For he would in practice be preaching to the proletariat confidence in the petty bourgeoisie ("this petty bourgeoisie, this peasantry, must separate itself from the bourgeoisie within the scope of the bourgeois-democratic revolution"). This would mean that for the sake of the "possibility" of a pleasant and sweet future, in which the peasantry would not form the tail of the bourgeoisie, in which the Socialists-Revolutionists, Chkheidze, Tsereteli and Steklov would not be an appendage of the bourgeois government,—that for the sake of the "possibility" of a pleasant future he would forget the unpleasant present in which the peasantry forms for the time being the tail of the bourgeoisie, in which the Socialists-Revolutionists and the Social-Democrats do not, for the time being, give up the rôle of an appendage of the bourgeois government, of the opposition of "His Majesty" Lvov.

This hypothetical person would resemble a saccharine Louis Blanc,* a sugary Kautskian, but in no way a revolutionary Marxist.

But are we not in danger of falling into subjectivism, of wanting to "skip" the bourgeois-democratic revolution—which has not yet been completed and has not gone through the peasant movement—and thus to arrive at the Socialist revolution?

This danger might threaten me, were I to say: "No Tsar, but a workers' government." But I have not said this, I have said something else. I have said that there can be no other government (barring a bourgeois one) in Russia except that of the Soviets of Workers', Agricultural Labourers', Soldiers' and Peasants' Deputies. I have said that, at present, power in Russia can pass from the Guchkovs and Lvovs *only* to these Soviets, in which it so happens that the majority are peasants, the majority are soldiers, the majority

* A French reformist Socialist who sided with the oppressors of the Paris Commune.—*Ed.*

42

are petty-bourgeois, using a scientific Marxian term, using not an everyday, philistine, professional, but a class characterisation.

In my theses, I have absolutely insured myself against any skipping of the peasant and other petty-bourgeois movements which are still in existence, against any *playing* with the "conquest of power" by a workers' government, against any kind of Blanquist * adventure, for I directly referred to the experiences of the Paris Commune. This experience, as is well known, and as was pointed out by Marx in 1871 and Engels in 1891, absolutely excluded Blanquism, absolutely secured direct, immediate and absolute rule of the *majority* and the activity of the masses only to the extent of the *conscious* action of the majority.

In the theses, I most definitely reduced the question to a struggle for influence within the Soviets of Workers', Agricultural Labourers', Soldiers' and Peasants' Deputies. In order to leave no trace of a doubt in this respect, I twice emphasised in the theses the necessity of patient, persistent work of "explaining," adapted to "the practical needs of the masses."

Ignorant persons or renegades from Marxism, such as Mr. Plekhanov and his ilk, may clamour about Anarchism, Blanquism, etc. Any one who wants to think and learn cannot fail to understand that Blanquism is seizure of power by a minority, whereas the Soviets of Workers' Deputies are admittedly the direct and immediate organisation of the majority of the people. Work reduced to a struggle for influence within such Soviets cannot, really cannot, drift into the swamp of Blanquism. It cannot drift into the swamp of Anarchism either, for Anarchism is a denial of the necessity of the state and state power for the epoch of transition from the rule of the bourgeoisie to the rule of the proletariat. Whereas I advocate, with a clearness that excludes any misunderstanding, the necessity of the state for this epoch, but, in accordance with Marx and with the experience of the Paris Commune, I advocate not the usual parliamentary bourgeois state, but a state without a standing army, without a police placed in opposition to the people, without an officialdom placed above the people.

When Mr. Plekhanov, in the newspaper *Yedinstvo*, inveighs with

---

* The teachings of the French revolutionist Auguste Blanqui (1805-1881) favouring the overthrow of the ruling power through secret plots of a few revolutionists rather than through preparation and organisation of the masses led by a revolutionary party.—*Ed.*

all his might against Anarchism, he only gives futher evidence of his breach with Marxism. In reply to my challenge in the *Pravda* (No. 26) that he relate what Marx and Engels taught about the state in the years 1871, 1872, 1875, Plekhanov can only answer with silence regarding the substance of the question and with a storm of abuse in the spirit of the embittered bourgeoisie.

Mr. Plekhanov, the ex-Marxist, has absolutely failed to understand the doctrine of Marxism about the state. Indeed, germs of this lack of understanding are also to be found in his German brochure on Anarchism.

Let us now see how Comrade L. Kamenev formulates his "disagreements" with my theses and with the above-expressed views in his short article in No. 27 of the *Pravda*. This will help us to clarify them with more exactness.

"As regards Comrade Lenin's general line," writes Comrade Kamenev, "it appears to us unacceptable, inasmuch as it proceeds from the assumption that the bourgeois-democratic revolution has been completed, and it builds on the immediate transformation of this revolution into a Socialist revolution."

There are two major errors in this.

1. The question of a "completed" bourgeois-democratic revolution is stated wrongly. The question is put in an abstract, simple, if we may say so, monochromatic way, which does not correspond to the objective reality. Any one who puts the question in this way, who *now* asks whether the bourgeois-democratic revolution has been completed, and nothing further, deprives himself of the possibility of seeing the extraordinarily complicated actuality which has at least two colours. This—in theory. In practice, he capitulates feebly to petty-bourgeois revolutionism.

As a matter of fact, reality shows us both the passing of the power into the hands of the bourgeoisie (a "completed" bourgeois-democratic revolution of the ordinary type) and, by the side of the actual government, the existence of a parallel government which represents the "revolutionary-democratic dictatorship of the proletariat and the peasantry." This latter "also government" has itself ceded power to the bourgeoisie, has voluntarily chained itself to the bourgeois government.

Is this reality embraced in the old Bolshevik formula of Comrade

Kamenev which says that "the bourgeois-democratic revolution is not completed"?

No, the formula is antiquated. It does not apply. It is dead. Attempts to revive it will be in vain.

2. A practical question. Who knows whether it is possible at present for a special "revolutionary-democratic dictatorship of the proletariat and the peasantry," detached from the bourgeois government, to exist in Russia? Marxian tactics must not be based on the unknown.

But if this is possible after all, then there is one, and only one way toward it, namely, a direct, resolute, irrevocable separation of the proletarian Communist elements from the petty-bourgeois elements.

Why?

Because the whole petty bourgeoisie has, not by chance but of necessity, turned towards chauvinism (defencism), towards "supporting" the bourgeoisie, towards depending on it, towards the fear of not getting on without it, etc.

How can the petty bourgeoisie be "pushed" into power, when this petty bourgeoisie could seize power *now*, but would not?

Only by separating the proletarian, the Communist Party, through proletarian class struggle free from the timidity of those petty-bourgeois, only by consolidating the proletarians who are free from the influence of the petty bourgeoisie in deed and not only in word—can one make things so "hot" for the petty bourgeoisie that, in certain circumstances, it will have to seize power; it is not even out of the question that Guchkov and Miliukov—again in certain circumstances —should stand for all power given solely to Chkheidze, Tsereteli, the Socialists-Revolutionists, Steklov, because after all they are all "defencists."

Any one who, right now, immediately and irrevocably, separates the proletarian elements of the Soviets (*i. e.*, the proletarian Communist Party) from the petty-bourgeois elements, provides a correct expression of the interests of the movement for either one of the two possible cases: for the case when Russia still goes through a special "dictatorship of the proletariat and the peasantry" independently of the bourgeoisie, and for the case when the petty bourgeoisie is not able to detach itself from the bourgeoisie and swings eternally (that is until Socialism is established) between us and it. Any one who is guided in his activities by the simple formula, "the bourgeois-democratic revolution is not completed," vouchsafes, as it were, the certainty of the petty bourgeoisie being independent of the bourgeoisie. In doing so, he at once helplessly surrenders to the petty bourgeoisie.

Apropos: With regard to the "formula" of the dictatorship of the proletariat and the peasantry, I would recall that, in my article "Two Tactics" (July, 1905) I specially emphasized (*Twelve Years,* p. 435):

> The revolutionary-democratic dictatorship of the proletariat and the peasantry has, like everything else in the world, a past and a future. Its past is absolutism, feudalism, monarchy, privileges. . . . Its future—the struggle against private property, the struggle of the wage-earners against the employers, the struggle for Socialism. . . .

The mistake made by Comrade Kamenev is that in 1917 he only sees the past of the revolutionary-democratic dictatorship of the proletariat and the peasantry. In reality, however, its future has already begun, for the interests and the policy of the wage-earners and the petty proprietors have already taken different lines, and that in such an important question as "defencism," the attitude toward the imperialist war.

This brings me to the second mistake in the remarks of Comrade Kamenev quoted above: He reproaches me, saying that my line "builds" on "the immediate transformation of this (bourgeois-democratic) revolution into a Socialist revolution."

This is not true. Not only do I not "build" on the "immediate transformation" of our revolution into a Socialist one, but I actually caution against it, when in Thesis No. 8, I state: "Not the 'introduction' of Socialism as an immediate task. . . ."

Is it not clear that any one who builds on the immediate transformation of our revolution into a Socialist one could not oppose the immediate task of introducing Socialism?

More than that. It is not even possible to introduce in Russia "immediately" a "commune state" (*i. e.,* a state organised according to the type of the Paris Commune), because for that it would be necessary that the majority of the Deputies in all (or in most) Soviets should clearly recognise the entire erroneousness and harm of the tactics and policy of the Socialists-Revolutionists, Chkheidze, Tsereteli, Steklov, etc. Whereas I declared in plain language that in this respect I only build on "patient" explaining (is it necessary to be patient to bring about a change which can be realised "immediately"?).

Comrade Kamenev has made a rather "impatient" start; he has repeated the bourgeois prejudice against the Paris Commune, namely, that it wanted to introduce Socialism "immediately." This is not true. The Commune, unfortunately, hesitated too long over the introduction of Socialism. The real essence of the Commune is not where the bourgeois usually look for it, but in the creation of a state of a special type. A state of this kind has already been born in Russia, it is the Soviets of Workers' and Soldiers' Deputies!

Comrade Kamenev has not grasped the fact, the significance of the existing Soviets, their identity, as to their socio-political character, with the Commune state; instead of studying the fact, he began to discuss what, in his opinion, I consider as the "immediate" future. The result is, unfortunately, a repetition of the method of many bourgeois: from the question as to what the Soviets of Workers' and Soldiers' Deputies are, whether they represent a higher type than a parliamentary republic, whether they are more useful for the people, more democratic, more adapted to the struggle, for instance, against the lack of bread, etc.,—from this urgent, real question raised by life itself, attention is diverted to the empty, allegedly scientific, in reality hollow, professionally lifeless question of "building on an immediate transformation."

An idle question put in the wrong way. I "build" only on this, exclusively on this—that the workers, soldiers and peasants will deal better than the officials, better than the police, with the practical, difficult problems of increasing the production of foodstuffs, their better distribution, the more satisfactory provisioning of the soldiers, etc., etc.

I am deeply convinced that the Soviets of Workers' and Soldiers' Deputies will make the independent activity of the people a reality more quickly and effectively than will a parliamentary republic (I will compare the two types of state in greater detail in another letter). They will more effectively, more practically and more correctly decide what steps can be taken toward Socialism and how these steps should be taken. Control over a bank, amalgamation of all banks into one, is not yet Socialism, but it is a step toward Socialism. To-day such steps are being taken in Germany by the Junkers and the bourgeoisie against the people. To-morrow the Soviet of Workers' and Soldiers' Deputies will be able to take these steps more effectively to the advantage of the people when the whole state power will be in its hands.

What compels the taking of such steps?

Famine. Economic disorganisation. Imminent collapse. War horrors. Horrors of the wounds inflicted on mankind by the war.

Comrade Kamenev concludes his article with the remark that "in a broad discussion he hopes to carry his point of view as the only possible one for revolutionary Social-Democracy in so far as it wishes to be and must remain to the very end the one and only party of the revolutionary masses of the proletariat without turning into a group of Communist propagandists."

It seems to me that these words betray a completely erroneous estimate of the situation. Comrade Kamenev contrasts a "party of the masses" with a "group of propagandists." Still, just now the "masses" have yielded to the frenzy of "revolutionary" defencism. Is it not more worthy of internationalists at this moment to be able to resist "mass" frenzy rather than to "wish to remain" with the masses, *i. e.*, to yield to the general epidemic? Have we not witnessed how in all the belligerent countries of Europe, the chauvinists justified themselves by their wish to "remain with the masses"? Is it not our duty to be able to remain for a while in the minority against a "mass" frenzy? Is not the work of the propagandists at the present moment the very central issue, since it tends to clear the proletarian line from the defencist and petty-bourgeois "mass" frenzy? It was just this fusion of the masses, proletarian and non-proletarian, without distinction of class differences inside of the masses, that formed one of the conditions for the defencist epidemic. To speak with contempt of a "group of propagandists" advocating a *proletarian* line does not seem to be very becoming.

Written in the middle of April, 1917.
First published in pamphlet form in 1917 by the "Priboi" publishing firm.